Your Spiritual Gifts Inventory

Charles V. Bryant

UPPER ROOM BOOKS®
NASHVILLE

Cover design: Bruce Gore/gorestudio.com

LIBRARY OF CONGRESS CATALOGING-IN-PUBLICATION DATA

Bryant, Charles V., 1930—
    Your spiritual gifts inventory / Charles V. Bryant.
        p. cm.
    ISBN 978-0-8358-0819-4
    1. Gifts, Spiritual. I. Title.
    BT767.3.B78   1997
234'.13—dc21   97-11416
                                                                CIP

Printed in the United States of America

GRACE-GIFTS DISCOVERY INVENTORY

Before you take this inventory, please consider four imperatives: (1) Pray sincerely for God's guidance. God wants you to know and use your gifts. (2) Do not relate these to your profession or occupation. (3) Do not consider how you relate to your family or what you do for your family. (4) Make every effort to rank all items *in relationship to* what you have done and experienced within the body of Christ, the church.

If you have no previous experience as a Christian or church member, consider this statement about each item: If I have the opportunity, time, and resources, this describes my inclination. (Then list one of the numbers described below.)

Rank each of the following statements according to how it describes your experience or strong inclination—not how to make you look good: *Much* (3), *Some* (2), *Little* (1), or *None* (0). Write the number of the value in the blank to the right of the statement.

1. I have a special sense of right and wrong, justice and injustice, and need to express it to others. _____

2. I enjoy working with and spiritually caring for groups of persons. _____

3. It is easy for me to aid persons in learning relevant information about the Bible and Christian living. _____

4. What I understand as divine truth is easy for me to apply to daily living. _____

5. Discovering or recognizing spiritual meanings and divine principles comes easily for me. _____

6. I delight in working with and encouraging depressed or apathetic persons. _____

7. I intuitively spot what is real or phony in other people and situations. _____

8. It is easy and enjoyable to manage my income so that I may give liberally to God's work. _____

9. The needs of others, more than my own or my family's, excite me to Christian action. _____

10. Persons with problems and pain attract my attention more quickly than others without apparent needs. _____

11. Other cultures, races, and languages offer no hurdles for my Christian service. _____

12. I bring persons to Christ through my personal efforts. _____

13. I offer friendship and other services to strangers without hesitation and fear. _____

14. I know God actively and purposely works in every event and circumstance. _____

15. I enjoy showing others how they can work for God in the church and the community. _____

16. I am energized by and feel joy when organizing a project, working out details, and getting others in the right places to reach a goal. _____

17. I feel that suffering is one of God's ways of accomplishing a divine purpose in life. _____

18. My prayers are a source of healing for others. _____

19. I pray in words or thoughts that I don't understand. _____

20. I understand and can interpret what others say or pray in words or phrases they do not know as a language. _____

21. Leaving the comforts of home, friends, and my church to serve other Christians elsewhere appeals to me. _____

22. Do I ever wonder how spiritually rewarding it must be not to be married? _____

23. I have a special sense of knowing when others need my prayers. _____

24. I am willing and able to endure any hardship to demonstrate God's love and power to others. _____

25. I enjoy doing most anything for the church and others as long as it serves Christ's purposes. _____

26. I sing praises to God with tunes I've never heard or learned. _____

27. I have a special sense about whether church buildings honor God and aid Christian discipleship. _____

28. When someone is an obvious victim of an alien evil desire, I feel a strong need to pray for that person's deliverance in the name of Jesus. _____

29. I enjoy debating persons who discredit the value of the church or Christian faith and usually win their esteem. _____

30. I enjoy making others laugh. _____

31. I become aware of surprisingly powerful results from some things I do for God's work. _____

32. A fulfilling life, to me, should be simple and free from obligations that do not directly support kingdom living. _____

33. Definite information and insights about personal and social evils come to me for correcting and guiding the church. _____

34. I enjoy being with and serving the same people over long periods of time. _____

35. I find it easy and enjoyable to explain what the New Testament teaches about Christian living. _____

36. What appears to be a complicated problem for others, I intuitively understand and solve. _____

37. I have special insights to God's will for the church and righteous living that do not always come from studying the Bible or from having a formal education. _____

38. I inspire and motivate others to do things for their spiritual well-being. _____

39. Something inside stirs me to question whether some things are from God, human nature, or evil. _____

40. Giving my time, talents, energy, and money is a cheerful experience of Christian living. _____

41. The main reason I do things for others is to help them in their spiritual growth. _____

42. I have immediate compassion for persons who have spiritual, emotional, or physical pain. _____

43. Ministering to persons who are different from me would be an exciting ministry. _____

44. I get great joy from telling persons who have not professed Christ as Savior how he became my Savior and how he wants to become theirs. _____

45. I sense a special opportunity for ministry when my normal routine is interrupted by guests or strangers. _____

46. I have a blessed assurance that God is involved in everything, small or great, and is working out a divine plan. _____

47. I seem to be "out front" of others in faith ventures, and many follow my example. _____

48. Organizing ideas, people, resources, and schedules is easy and enjoyable for me. _____

49. I identify my pains and tragedies as sharing the suffering of our Lord. _____

50. Because of my specific prayers, certain unhealthy conditions change for the good. _____

51. I experience a spiritual presence and power when I pray or chant in a wordless form. _____

52. When others deliver inspired messages in words and sounds not known by the hearers, I am able to explain. _____

53. I yearn to go to new places to proclaim Christ and to help establish another group of believers. _____

54. I can be a whole person outside a social or legal bond with one person. _____

55. When I hear requests for prayers, I eagerly and immediately begin to pray. _____

56. The prospect of loss or gain because of my faith in Jesus Christ causes me no abiding concern. _____

57. I do most anything that needs to be done because everything is an opportunity to glorify God. _____

58. I easily discern when music is a performance rather than a spiritual aid to worship. _____

59. I recognize that religious symbols are essential for enhancing Christian fellowship and worship. _____

60. I know when there are conflicts between evil and good forces, and I feel that God wants to use me to eradicate the evil. _____

61. I have such strong feelings about the rightness of the church's role in the affairs of life that I stand ready to defend it at whatever cost. _____

62. It is easy for me to spot humor in most situations, even serious and painful ones. _____

63. I feel mysteriously connected to a divine power when doing ministries of Christ for others. _____

64. I enjoy having a minimal income and no debts so that my interests and energies may be put to Christ's use. _____

65. I am stirred by the modern relevance of biblical teachings and principles and must speak my mind about them. _____

66. I find it easy and enjoyable to sustain deep relationships with a variety of people. _____

67. I devote much time to biblical and spiritual studies to share with others. _____

68. When I am faced with several options, my choices result in positive effects. _____

69. I understand and can connect different Bible stories and teachings without difficulty. _____

70. I consider it important that others gain strength and comfort from my ministries. _____

71. I am deeply disturbed when something seems wrong and exuberant over what seems right without any apparent reason for my judgment; eventually, my feelings prove correct. _____

72. When there is a call for donations, I feel excited enough to do all I can. _____

73. Doing routine tasks is not dull or drudgery for me if it helps others in their spiritual journey. _____

74. Doing something for persons in nursing homes, hospitals, hospices, and other caregiving places satisfies me greatly. _____

75. I have something of value to contribute to people in socioeconomic, racial, or language situations radically different from mine. _____

76. I have deeper feelings for people who need to know Christ as Savior than for regular church members who already know Christ. _____

77. I make strangers and newcomers comfortable in my presence. _____

78. To me, God's will is more important than either a deliverance from the unpleasant or an acquisition of the wonderful. _____

79. I have dreams and visions of new ministries that the church can offer, and I enjoy helping to set long-range goals for the church's ministries. _____

80. When I take on projects, my planning, detailing, and supervising result in people friendliness and smooth operation. _____

81. I see God's powerful love in my sorrow, hardships, pain, or loss. _____

82. God heals the physically, mentally, socially, financially, or spiritually sick through my efforts. _____

83. I feel spiritually right and normal to pray or to give praise to God with utterances unlike any language I know. _____

84. I delight in understanding and translating for others who speak with unintelligible words. _____

85. People accept what I say about spiritual matters without offering rebuttals. _____

86. The divine purpose of singleness is freedom to give more time to ministries for our Lord and his church. _____

87. Praying is my most enjoyable spiritual activity. _____

88. I am stubborn and unyielding in my insistence on what Christ means to me and to everyone. _____

89. I think of cleaning, clerical work, caring for buildings, ushering, babysitting, mowing, setting up chairs, and other acts as significant ways to worship God. _____

90. My music becomes a God-given means for preparing souls for a special anointing of grace. _____

91. I feel a special closeness to God when I build, make, or repair something related to the church and God's people. _____

92. At times I feel that my praying is a battlefield on which evil and good forces are battling for control over someone or some event. _____

93. I feel like a Christian soldier at war with evil, not people. _____

94. I experience fun and entertainment as vital parts of the practice of Christian faith. _____

95. Though I do not intend it, extraordinary things occur when I assert special efforts for Christ and his church. _____

96. God does not want me to have worldly possessions, so that the kingdom may claim my time and strength. _____

97. I experience urges to speak God's message that prove to be timely and needed by others. _____

98. I find it easy to carry a large number of concerns for many persons with a variety of needs. _____

99. I enjoy arduous and long hours of study to make God's word plain and easy to understand for others. _____

100. The themes of love, righteousness, holiness, peace, and discipleship are easy for me to translate into practical acts of daily Christian living. _____

101. Meanings and overtones of biblical themes are more important than mere facts, names, or dates. _____

102. I urge others to believe their sufferings and trials will develop their patience, strength, and hope. _____

103. I easily detect spiritual truth and error when others see no cause to question the difference. _____

104. I do not care how the church uses my contributions, since what I give is unto God. _____

105. I am satisfied just to serve others, even if I never get recognized for what I do. _____

106. I actually feel the discomforts and pains of others, and I get relief only by doing something to relieve theirs. _____

107. I daydream about living and serving God among people of other nations, races, and cultures. _____

108. I believe that the primary purpose of the church is to win persons to Christ. _____

109. I really love meeting new people and learning about them, and I am eager to greet them to make them feel welcome. _____

110. I know God is real; though circumstances appear hard, cruel, and impossible to others, I relax in knowing that God is in control. _____

111. Others say that my influence has guided them to gain new directions and achievements in life. _____

112. All ministries should be amply planned, sufficiently staffed, and carried out to the fullest detail. _____

113. God uses my sorrows to bring about radical changes for the good of other persons and events. _____

114. Through my counseling, touch, or prayer, illnesses disappear. _____

115. In my private devotions, I pray both with words I understand and with utterances I don't understand. _____

116. I interpret messages from spiritual languages to build up the members of the church. _____

117. I enjoy spending lots of time visiting other churches to aid them in their services to Christ. _____

118. God gives special relief from sexual needs and frustrations to single persons. _____

119. I am moved to pray for others, even though I may not know them, and for conditions about which I know very little or nothing at the time. _____

120. I prefer dying painfully for Jesus Christ than dying painlessly without knowing him personally. _____

121. Because of a special closeness I feel to God when I do any kind of work for the church, I am quick to volunteer. _____

122. When I sing or play music, I feel spiritual energy flowing through me. _____

123. I am spiritually fulfilled when engaged in creative and artistic physical or manual work for the good of the church. _____

124. I need to know and to name the demonic force in order to pray or work effectively for its elimination. _____

125. I view the church as an army of the Lord and myself as a part of its special victory force. _____

126. I recognize amusing events and statements in the Bible that most people do not see. _____

127. I experience unexpected and unsolicited inner promptings to do some service for Christ and the church and learn later of unbelievable results. _____

128. I feel it is important for me to identify with the poor to build their confidence in my service to them. _____

129. I receive special insights for warnings, cautions, instructions, and encouragements to give to the church for its effectiveness and preservation. _____

130. I have special feelings for Christians who have strayed and for church members who are inactive. _____

131. It gives me pleasure to explain God's word in such a way that others learn how to live righteously. _____

132. I see God's will clearly and how to apply it to personal living and church ministries. _____

133. It is clear to me how biblical teachings relate to universal and timeless needs of human life. _____

134. Through my personal involvement, troubled, depressed, or confused persons receive strength and composure in the Lord. _____

135. I have a special sensing for false teachings, erroneous judgments, and insincere and dishonest behavior. _____

136. My giving as a Christian is determined not by my special interests, ability, or resources but by joy and gratitude. _____

137. People are so important to me that everything I do as a Christian must be done for their good. _____

138. I have strong inclinations toward people with troubles and special needs, and I get special joy from helping them. _____

139. My heart goes out to the unchurched, underprivileged, and others the church is not touching with its gospel of Christ. _____

140. While talking with anyone who appears not to be a Christian, I experience a strong desire to be the one to win him or her to Christ. _____

141. I do not mind and am not afraid to welcome unknown persons into my home. _____

142. Even when wrong prevails and situations threaten with hopelessness, I sense that God's blessing is forthcoming. _____

143. People seek me out to lead them in their faith ventures. _____

144. Carrying the responsibility for organizing group activities toward stated goals is something I enjoy and do well. _____

145. My witness in affliction and trouble has been used by God to lead others to experience the joy of Christ in their hardships. _____

146. Directly through my various efforts, healings occurred that did not come from natural or medical means. _____

147. Praying or praising God in wordless sounds and phrases gives me a sense of unhindered and intimate communication with God. _____

148. I receive direct clarifications of divine messages for the good of the church through persons who, to others, speak in unintelligible gibberish.   _____

149. When I visit from church to church and have occasion to speak, I feel a sense of authority in spiritual matters that comes only from God.   _____

150. Being single and enjoying it never discounts the value of marriage for others but frees me to serve the church more fully.   _____

151. I feel urges to pray for others to be empowered for effective ministries.   _____

152. Whatever the costs, I do not hesitate to tell others about God's love in Jesus Christ.   _____

153. It does not matter how menial or mundane my task; my joy is doing it for Christ.   _____

154. I can tell whether certain hymns and types of music are spiritually suitable for the occasion.   _____

155. Engaging my manual skills for Christ and his church is a special form of prayer and ministry for me.   _____

156. God uses my obedience to free others of evil forces.   _____

157. I think of unbelievers not as enemies but as persons in need of a strong Christian influence and commander.   _____

158. I use wholesome jokes and laughable statements to relieve others of pressure, anxiety, or suffering.   _____

159. I feel mystically empowered by the presence of God when doing some things that others may consider insignificant, strange, or impossible. _____

160. Having little of this world's goods doesn't make me feel inferior to others or left out of God's grace. _____

HOW TO SCORE YOUR INVENTORY

The numbers in the chart on the next page refer to the numbered inventory items you just ranked. Look back at the inventory to see the value you assigned to each question, and pencil in that value (3, 2, 1, or 0) next to the number of that question in each box. After listing the 160 values, add your total horizontally for each row in the chart. (Do not include the printed numbers.) Put the sum on the line in the Total column. The sum ranges from 0 to 15.

The total for each row indicates the extent to which you may be gifted or inclined to operate the gift named in the first column of the row. Look to see which gifts have the highest totals. If you recorded a high total for the gift of evangelism, for example, you might pray for ways God can best help you operate that gift. Read Chapter 13, "Discovering Our Gifts," for more clues as to what you do to fully utilize your gift.

The Inventory Scoring Chart is on the next page.

Gifts	Values					Total
Prophecy	1	33	65	97	129	
Pastor	2	34	66	98	130	
Teaching	3	35	67	99	131	
Wisdom	4	36	68	100	132	
Knowledge	5	37	69	101	133	
Exhortation	6	38	70	102	134	
Discernment	7	39	71	103	135	
Giving	8	40	72	104	136	
Helps	9	41	73	105	137	
Mercy	10	42	74	106	138	
Missionary	11	43	75	107	139	
Evangelism	12	44	76	108	140	
Hospitality	13	45	77	109	141	
Faith	14	46	78	110	142	
Leadership	15	47	79	111	143	
Administration	16	48	80	112	144	
Suffering	17	49	81	113	145	
Healings	18	50	82	114	146	
Prayer Language	19	51	83	115	147	
Interpretation	20	52	84	116	148	
Apostle	21	53	85	117	149	
Singleness	22	54	86	118	150	
Intercessory Prayer	23	55	87	119	151	
Martyrdom	24	56	88	120	152	
Service	25	57	89	121	153	
Spirit-Music	26	58	90	122	154	
Craftsmanship	27	59	91	123	155	
Exorcism	28	60	92	124	156	
Battle	29	61	93	125	157	
Humor	30	62	94	126	158	
Miracles	31	63	95	127	159	
Poverty	32	64	96	128	160	

GIFTS' DEFINITIONS
AND BIBLICAL REFERENCES

These definitions have been kept to a minimum number of words. Elaborations are available in the chapters describing the gifts. Keep in mind the adjective *extraordinary*, which should be placed before the word *ability*. Spiritual gifts are superabilities God gives for ministries.

1. *Prophecy.* The ability to link biblical truths and God's will for today's living and to be an instrument for revealing or interpreting historic or current messages from God for righteous and just living in today's world.

Acts 2:14-36; 11:28; 15:32; 21:10ff.; 21:9-11
Romans 12:6
1 Corinthians 12:10; 14:3, 6, 24ff.
Ephesians 3:1-6; 4:11-14

2. *Pastor.* The ability to carry varieties of spiritual, physical, and social concerns for groups and individuals and to persist over long periods of time and circumstances with effective caring.

Matthew 18:12-14	Ephesians 4:11-14
John 10:1-30	1 Timothy 3:1-7
Acts 20:28	1 Peter 5:2-4

3. *Teaching.* The ability to discern, analyze, and deliver biblical and other spiritual truths to help others to comprehend and accept the clear calling of God to live justly and righteously.

Acts 13:1; 18:24-28; 20:20-21   1 Timothy 2:7
1 Corinthians 12:28   2 Timothy 1:11
Ephesians 4:11   James 3:1

4. *Wisdom.* The ability to make concrete, practical, and specific applications of divine knowledge received directly from God, from one's spiritual gift of knowledge, or from another's shared gift or gifts.

Acts 6:3, 10; 7:10   Colossians 1:28; 3:16
1 Corinthians 1:18-27;   2 Peter 3:15
     3:18-19; 12:18

5. *Knowledge.* The ability to ascertain and to understand the universal and timeless truths of God and to link them with the church in its mission through Christ for justice and righteousness in the world.

Acts 5:1-11   2 Corinthians 11:6
Romans 11:33   Ephesians 3:19
1 Corinthians 12:8   Colossians 2:3

6. *Exhortation.* The ability to counsel, inspire, motivate, encourage, and strengthen others in and through their efforts to live out God's will and calling as Christians in pain or pleasure, want or plenty.

Acts 4:36; 11:19-26; 14:22   1 Timothy 4:13
Romans 12:8   Hebrews 10:25
1 Thessalonians 2:11

7. *Discerning of Spirits.* The ability to differentiate between good and evil, right and wrong, and what is of God, human nature, or evil, and to use this knowledge for the protection and health of the body of Christ.

Matthew 7:6	2 Peter 2:1-3
Acts 5:1-11; 8:22-23	1 John 4:1-6
1 Corinthians 12:10	

8. *Giving.* The ability to manage one's resources of income, time, energy, and skills to exceed what is considered to be a reasonable standard for giving to the church, an amount that brings joy and power to do more for further service.

1 Kings 17:8-16	Acts 4:32-37
Mark 12:41-44	Romans 12:8
Luke 8:1-3; 21:1-4	2 Corinthians 8:1-7

9. *Helps.* The ability and eagerness to aid or assist others in need to such an extent that the helper receives as much as the persons helped.

Psalm 21:1	Acts 9:36
Mark 15:41	Romans 16:1-2
Luke 8:2-3	1 Corinthians 12:28

10. *Mercy.* The ability to identify with and actually feel the physical, mental, spiritual, and emotional pain or distress of others and to feel the absolute necessity to do something to relieve them.

Matthew 20:29-34	Acts 11:28-30; 16:33-34
Mark 9:41	Romans 12:8
Luke 10:33-35	

11. *Missionary.* The ability to go beyond race, culture, subculture, creeds, nationality, or lifestyle to serve the basic human and spiritual needs of certain neglected peoples.

Matthew 25:37-40; 28:19-20   Romans 10:14-17
Acts 8:4-8; 13:2-12   1 Corinthians 9:19-23

12. *Evangelism.* The ability to give such a persuasive witness to the love of God as expressed in Jesus Christ that it moves others to accept that love and to become disciples of Christ.

Acts 8:5-6; 21:8   1 Timothy 2:7
1 Corinthians 3:5-6   2 Timothy 4:5
Ephesians 4:11

13. *Hospitality.* The ability to extend caring and sharing to persons (strangers) beyond one's intimate circle to demonstrate and establish the unlimited and inclusive companionship of Christ.

Matthew 25:35   1 Timothy 3:2
Acts 16:14-16   Titus 1:8
Romans 12:13   1 Peter 4:9-10

14. *Faith.* The ability to extend one's basic or saving faith to serve corporate or individual needs specifically related to the life and ministry of the church, the body of Christ.

Matthew 17:19-21   Romans 4:18-21
Mark 9:23   1 Corinthians 12:9
Acts 11:22-24   Hebrews 11

15. *Leadership* The ability to envision God's will and purpose for the church and to demonstrate compelling skills in capturing the imaginations, energies, skills, and spiritual gifts of others to pursue and accomplish God's will.

Luke 10:16   1 Timothy 3:4; 5:17
Acts 7:10   Titus 3:8, 14
Romans 12:8   Hebrews 13:17

16. *Administration.* The ability to sort out resources and persons for effective church ministries and to organize and implement them into ministry projects until completion with eventful results.

Luke 14:28-30   Romans 12:8
Acts 6:1-7   1 Corinthians 12:28

17. *Suffering.* The ability to endure hardship, pain, and distress with an amount of joy and fortitude to inspire others to endure their suffering and to lead others to accept God's offer of salvation made possible in Christ's suffering.

Matthew 16:24   2 Corinthians 11:23-27;
Mark 8:34   12:1-10
John 18:11   Philippians 1:29ff.
Romans 8:17   1 Peter 4:12-14

18. *Healings.* The ability to cure or to be cured of ill conditions that hinder effective ministries for Christ, the church, or individuals.

Luke 5:17; 6:19; 9:2, 11, 42   1 Corinthians 12:9, 28
Acts 3:1-10; 5:12-16   1 Peter 2:24

19. *Prayer-Praise Language.* The ability to pray or to praise God with beneficial wordless phrases or utterances not familiar as a known language, and with such a joy-filled intimacy with Christ that faith is strengthened and ministries become effective.

Acts 2:1-13; 10:44-46; 19:1-7   1 Corinthians 12:10, 28; 13:1;
Romans 8:26-27   14:4-5, 22
Ephesians 6:18

20. *Interpretation.* The ability to hear, comprehend, and translate spiritual messages given by others in wordless phrases or utterances unfamiliar as a known language or to decipher and translate spiritual messages from another who speaks in a known language but not recognized by the interpreter.

Luke 24:27   1 Corinthians 12:10, 30; 14:5,
Acts 2:14-21   13, 27

21. *Apostle.* The ability to adhere to the personality of Jesus Christ and his tradition of missional itineracy so that one may wield effective spiritual oversight of new people in new places for the purpose of extending Christian ministries for spiritual, just, and righteous living.

Acts 15:1-2   Galatians 2:1-10
1 Corinthians 12:28   Ephesians 3:1-13; 4:11
2 Corinthians 12:12

22. *Singleness.* The ability to offer God and the church a life free from marriage, family responsibilities, and sexual frustrations to spend time and energies necessary for certain Christian ministries.

Isaiah 56:3-5   1 Corinthians 7:7, 27-28, 32-35
Matthew 19:10-12; 22:27-30

23. *Intercessory Prayer.* The ability to know when, and for whom or what to pray with effective results.

Luke 22:41-44   Colossians 1:9-12; 4:12-13
Acts 12:5, 12; 16:25-26   1 Timothy 2:1; 4:5
Romans 8:26-27   James 5:14-18

24. *Martyrdom.* The ability to stand firm on divinely inspired convictions and divinely directed ministries without equivocation or ulterior motives.

Acts 6:10, 15; 7:54-60   1 Thessalonians 2:2
1 Corinthians 13:3   1 Timothy 6:12

25. *Service.* The ability to elevate any deed or service that aids the church or another person to a form of worship without concern or desire for rank, popularity, position, or recognition.

Matthew 4:11   Acts 6:1
Mark 1:31   Romans 12:7
Luke 10:40   Galatians 6:2, 10
John 12:2   Titus 3:4

26. *Spirit-Music.* The ability to create or perform lyrics and musical tunes as messages from God to inspire others to Christian service, to win others to Christ, or to tell the story of God's love and grace.

2 Chronicles 5:11-14   1 Corinthians 14:15
Psalm 57:7-9   Ephesians 5:19

27. *Craftsmanship.* The ability to use physical materials and artistic skills to create, mold, carve, sculpt, draw, design, paint, repair, or photograph items necessary for spiritual nurture, faith development, and caring ministries.

Exodus 35:20-35; 36:1-3

28. *Exorcism.* The ability to use faith, prayers, spirit-music, or other spiritual gifts to liberate persons from debilitating and hindering forces and evil circumstances to free them to use their gifts effectively to serve the body of Christ and others through the church.

1 Samuel 16:14-23   Acts 5:16; 8:6-8; 16:16; 19:11-12
Matthew 8:16-17; 12:43-45   1 Corinthians 2:6-8; 10:20-21
Mark 1:24; 16:17   Ephesians 6:10-18
Luke 9:1, 49-50; 10:17; 11:25   Colossians 1:13-15; 2:20

29. *Battle.* The ability to use spiritual, physical, or psychological energies with righteous force enough to confront and overcome evil that hinders the church's mission to do God's will.

Deuteronomy 31:6   1 Corinthians 16:13
Joshua 1:6-9   Ephesians 6:10-17
2 Samuel 10:12   1 Thessalonians 2:2
Daniel 10:19   1 Timothy 6:12
Acts 23:11

30. *Humor.* The ability to bring laughter and joy to situations and relationships to relieve tension, anxiety, or conflict and to heal and free emotions and energies needed for effective ministries.

John 13:6-15   Galatians 5:12
1 Corinthians 12:12-24

31. *Miracles.* The ability to do powerful works that transcend our perception of natural laws and means to free the church or individuals from conditions that restrict needed ministries.

Genesis 18:14   Acts 4:30; 5:1-10, 12; 13:11
Mark 9:38-40; 16:17-18   1 Corinthians 2:4; 12:10, 28
Luke 1:37

32. *Voluntary Poverty.* The ability to live a simple, conservative, and unencumbered life free of material responsibilities in order to devote large amounts of time, energy, and skills to essential ministries.

Mark 1:18, 20; 10:21   1 Corinthians 13:3
Acts 2:45; 4:34-35   2 Corinthians 8:9